What if animals co...

They can in . . .

The SUPER SECRET

A Tale about Wisdom

Written and illustrated by

T. F. Marsh

Faith Kids

Equipping Kids for Life!

*S*haboom! Howdy, friend. My name's Mr. Boom. I'm a power-punching, mega-muscle super skunk. But ya' know, things weren't always this way. I was once a skinny, bare-boned skunkeroo. Then a feller named Samson showed me how to become packed with power. Let this Tale Teller pass this old tale straight down to you.

One mornin' long ago, a wild wind came blastin' through my family's mountain home. I was carried far away and dropped down in a strange land. I looked up to find a little striped bee starin' back at me. And that's where it all began.

H owdy," I said, friendly like to that little gal. "My name's Dergal." (That was my name back then.)

"I'm Honeycomb," she buzzed back. "Have you come to see Mr. Samson too?"

"Who's Mr. Samson?" I asked.

She rolled her eyes. "Why, he's *only* the strongest man alive. We ladies love him. C'mon, silly. I'll show him to you."

Honeycomb led me to a small town. As we entered through the gate, there he was: Mr. Samson. *Shaboom!* Ladies surrounded him as he flexed his muscles. Why, even his *hair* looked strong.

"Isn't he a dream?" sighed Honeycomb.

"Yeah, I reckon," I answered, "but how did he get so strong?"

She flew up close and buzzed in my ear, "It's a super secret."

L et me explain," she continued. "Long ago, the angel of the Lord visited the wife of Manoah of Zorah. The angel told her that her future son would rescue Israel from the evil Philistines! He was to be dedicated to the Lord and follow all the ways of the Nazirite life. And that included one special instruction: no haircuts. *That's* why he's so strong."

Well, that day I saw something I wanted: power, and lots of it. So I began bodybuilding. Day and night I worked out to get stronger than Samson. And, of course, I grew my *own* super hair. Finally, I was ready. I had become the strongest skunk alive. I had become . . . Mr. Boom!

One day I followed Samson to Timnah, where he spotted a beautiful Philistine girl. He decided right then that he wanted to marry her.

Back home, Samson told his folks. They disapproved. They wanted him to settle down with an Israelite girl. But Samson would only have that Philistine, so back he went with his parents to collect his future wife.

As we neared Timnah, a lion suddenly attacked. Right before my eyes, Samson became filled with super strength. *Shaboom!* Using his bare hands, he tore up that old lion. Critters gathered from all around, amazed.

"Ah, that was nothin'," I boasted as I quickly fashioned my own lion punching bag. Then . . . *boom!* I tore up that old rag doll.

It sat there stiller than a heron waitin' for a bullfrog.

Well, soon the wedding plans were set.

Travelin' back to Timnah for the wedding, we passed that old dead lion. But now its carcass was full of bees and honey. Even little Honeycomb was buzzin' inside!

"Shucks, this stuff is too gooey for me," I griped after grabbin' a helping.

But gooey fingers didn't matter to Samson. Why, he just stuck his hands in that critter and pulled out a big gob of honey! That honey gave him an idea.

At his wedding feast, Samson held a contest. His guests had seven days to answer a riddle and win new clothes! The riddle was:

Out of the eater came something to eat;
out of the strong came something sweet.

A s I watched the puzzled guests, a snooty fox came waltzin' over to me.

"Excuse me, good sir," he said with his snout in the air. "Archibald Rustail is the name, and intellect is my game. May I inquire your thoughts on that odd riddle. I mean, what kind of riddle is *that?*"

"It's one they'll never answer," I shot back.

But the wedding guests threatened to kill Samson's wife and her family if she didn't tell them the answer. Day after day she cried and begged Samson for the answer. That gal began wearing him down.

Finally, on the last day of the contest, he told her. And soon that gal told *everyone. Even* ol' Rustail. The guests returned to Samson with the answer:

What is sweeter than honey?
What is stronger than a lion?

*S*amson became mighty angry and left in a huff. After he returned with their prizes, he turned and marched straight home.

But he only needed a little time to cool off. He began missin' his new wife. And so, once again, it was back to Timnah. And back for more trouble.

When we arrived, Samson was in for a surprise. Ya' see, thinkin' he wasn't coming back, his wife had married another man. *Shaboom!* Now Samson was *really* angry! We marched straight out to the Philistine wheat fields. Samson tied together in pairs the tails of three hundred foxes and fastened a torch to each pair of tails. Then he set those foxes loose! Why, even ol' Rustail was a-yalpin'!

I, of course, could outdo that! So ... *boom!* I started my own fire with little old fireflies. They were hotter than lightning splittin' through an old hollow log!

A s those fields burned up we retreated to the rocks of Etam. That's where I met that old hermit, Lyle Lilapad.

"Did you know that the Philistines have surrounded the men of Judah?" he cracked. "Your friend Samson's to blame."

He was right. To avoid trouble for his people, Samson agreed to be bound and handed over to the Philistines.

Those Philistines, though, began bothering him while he was all tied up. Suddenly, Samson was filled with super strength. *Shaboom!* With a donkey's jawbone, he whomped a thousand Philistine warriors!

Now, as those Philistines fell dead, two thousand flies showed up. So, I grabbed old Lyle's wooden cane. Now I had my *own* weapon. A handy-dandy fly swatter! Then . . . *boom!* I began swingin'.

Those ugly fellers fell faster than a hummin' bird who'd lost his propellers!

Well, friend, I could continue tellin' more heroic stories, but the point is we were unstoppable! Well, almost.

Ya' see, everything was going super until the day we wandered into the valley of Sorek. There, Samson fell in love again. This time to a gal named Ms. Delilah. Why, even *she* had long hair. And so did her pretty little neighbor. *Shaboomboomboom!* I moseyed over and introduced myself. "Howdy, pretty gal," I said, sighing. "I'm Mr. Boom. I'm very pleased to meet ya'."

She turned and scrunched her nose.

"Pleasure's all mine," she responded. "I'm Ms. Sweet-flower." *Gulp!* Now *I* was in love! That female had me snagged tighter than a crawdad in a fishin' net.

A short time later, the leaders of the Philistines came to visit Delilah privately. They offered her money to find out the secret of Samson's super strength.

Now Delilah loved to play games, and she included Samson in all of them. In each game, Delilah asked him about his super secret. Where did his strength come from? How could he be bound and subdued? Three times she tied him up. Three times she shouted that the Philistines were there. Three times he broke free and spoiled her fun. Finally, Delilah became frustrated. And so did Ms. Sweetflower. "What kind of secret is this?" Ms. Sweetflower huffed.

"It's one Delilah will never get," I proudly answered.

O nce again there was crying. Day after day Delilah nagged for the answer. She said Samson didn't love her. Finally, he told her the secret: no haircuts. If he disobeyed the Lord's special instructions, no super strength.

"Shucks," I said. "Here we go again."

Delilah grinned. Now she knew Samson's super secret.

What happened next is shocking, but ya'll need to hear it. Not long after this, Samson fell sound asleep with his head on Delilah's lap. All was still as she began strokin' his hair. Then, quiet-like, Delilah turned and called in the lords of the Philistines. She told them she had what they wanted: the super secret.

"What are *they* doing here?" I asked Ms. Sweetflower.

Ms. Sweetflower smiled and cuddled up next to me. "Just watch," she whispered. "Delilah has a *super surprise* for Samson."

She was right! The Philistines paid Delilah the silver they had promised her. And while Samson slept, they cut his hair with a razor.

Then Delilah shouted that the Philistines were there! Yawnin', Samson woke up. No problem. Shucks, he would spoil her fun just as always.

But this time, his super strength was gone. He didn't know that the Lord had left him. Delilah held up Samson's cut hair. Then those nasty Philistines grabbed him, blinded his eyes, and dragged him away. He didn't look too proud anymore.

As I hung my head, Ms. Sweetflower began strokin' *my* hair.

"Oh, Mr. Boom," she cooed, "come take a rest on *my* lap."

Shaboom! Now *she* was holdin' the razor!

"No haircut for me!" I yelled.

I flew out of there quicker than a sparrow bein' chased by a hickory hawk!

Time passed slowly after that sad day. Samson was now a Philistine prisoner grinding grain. As for me, life had become boring. There was nobody to compete against. Nobody to outdo. I twiddled my thumbs as my super life faded away. My three friends would come by and try to cheer up this poor old hero.

"Go punch out another homespun kitty," buzzed Honeycomb.

"Go light up another wheat field," suggested Rustail.

"Go swat another thousand flies," begged Lyle.

I sighed. "Boring. Boring. Boring. I've done all that stuff before. Why should I do it again? Life's just plain boring."

With nothing to do, we decided to take a stroll over to the Philistine temple in Gaza. It sounded as if someone was at least having fun over there.

Yep. The place was packed with Philistines! They were havin' a huge party while worshiping their god Dagon. And the main attraction was . . . Samson! Why, they were all laughin' at that poor, blind, long-haired prisoner.

But wait! His hair was back. Longer than ever. If he hadn't been blind, he would have crushed those Philistines.

And yet, maybe he *could* see . . . maybe better than before. Ya' see, Samson had changed. This time, he *humbly* asked the Lord for His super strength. One last time he wanted to defeat the Philistines. And the Lord heard and answered his prayer. *Shaboom!* His super strength returned. Samson began pushin' on two pillars holdin' up the roof. The ceiling and walls began to crack and crumble. This place was comin' down!

We hightailed it out of there as fast as Mr. Boom could zoom! *KABOOM!!!*

That day, Samson destroyed more Philistines than he had in his whole life. Sadly, Samson's life ended that day too. He had judged Israel for twenty years.

It wasn't till after he was buried that I understood the *real* secret to his super strength. Ya' see, it wasn't in his hair—it came from the Lord's Spirit! Because Samson *broke* his vow of no haircuts, the Lord *kept* His vow of no super strength. Shucks! It was all in the vow. *Shaboom.*

So now *I'm* the strongest in the land! Nobody comes close to me. No foolin'. Nobody! Ya' see, with my super strength has also come a super smell. And for anyone near *this* super skunk . . . that's trouble.

Now that we've imagined how it might be if animals could tell us their tales, go ahead and read God's account of this story in your Bible. You'll find it in Judges 13:1–16:31.

Faith Kids® is an imprint of Cook Communications Ministries,
Colorado Springs, Colorado 80918
Cook Communications, Paris, Ontario
Kingsway Communications, Eastbourne, England

THE SUPER SECRET
© 2001 by T. F. Marsh for text and illustrations

ISBN: 0-7814-3519-6

Designed by Dana Sherrer of iDesignEtc.
Edited by Kathy Davis

First printing, 2001
Printed in Canada
05 04 03 02 01   5 4 3 2 1

Faith Parenting Guide

Ages 4-7

Wisdom

The Super Secret

Ages: 4-7

My child's need: To learn to make wise choices

Biblical value: Wisdom

Learning styles: Help your child learn about
making wise choices in the following ways:

Sight: Have your child point to the different pictures of Samson in the book. For each, ask, "Was Samson following and obeying God?" Point out that God's rules serve an important purpose, and they can keep us out of trouble. When we break His rules, we suffer, just as Samson did when he lost his strength.

Sound: After reading the story aloud to your child, talk about Samson's wisdom (or lack of it) when:
• Samson gave his wedding guests seven days to answer a riddle, then at the last minute told the answer to his wife who immediately informed everybody else.
• Samson used foxes to burn the Philistines' wheat fields.
• Samson told Delilah the secret of his super strength.
• Samson humbly asked the Lord for strength.
Explain that Samson was wise when he obeyed God and foolish when he made his own choices.

Touch: Have your child build a tower of wooden blocks. Then see if he or she can remove blocks from the bottom. Of course, the tower will fall over. Explain that Samson's strength was built on God's power, just like the tower was standing on a strong foundation of blocks. When God's power was gone, Samson could not be strong. Emphasize that even though Samson fell, God gave him one more chance to show wisdom.